Reincarnate
NOW!

Yesterday's Storms Can Create
Tomorrow's Rainbows

Allen M. Daugherty

BALBOA.PRESS
A DIVISION OF HAY HOUSE

This book is a work of non-fiction. Unless otherwise noted, the author
and the publisher make no explicit guarantees as to the accuracy of
the information contained in this book and in some cases, names
of people and places have been altered to protect their privacy.

Balboa Press books may be ordered through booksellers or by contacting:

Balboa Press
A Division of Hay House
1663 Liberty Drive
Bloomington, IN 47403
www.balboapress.com
844-682-1282

Because of the dynamic nature of the Internet, any web addresses or
links contained in this book may have changed since publication and
may no longer be valid. The views expressed in this work are solely those
of the author and do not necessarily reflect the views of the publisher,
and the publisher hereby disclaims any responsibility for them.

The author of this book does not dispense medical advice or prescribe
the use of any technique as a form of treatment for physical, emotional,
or medical problems without the advice of a physician, either directly
or indirectly. The intent of the author is only to offer information
of a general nature to help you in your quest for emotional and
spiritual well-being. In the event you use any of the information in
this book for yourself, which is your constitutional right, the author
and the publisher assume no responsibility for your actions.

Print information available on the last page.

ISBN: 978-1-9822-5809-2 (sc)
ISBN: 978-1-9822-5808-5 (e)

Balboa Press rev. date: 11/05/2020

CONTENTS

PREFACE

BEFORE YOU GET too far into this book, let's chat a bit. First, if you are looking for a book on the actual beliefs of Reincarnation, this is not one of those. Yes, I know, it is the title of the book but you will see that we are discussing a figurative type of reincarnating as opposed to a literal one. I promise by the time you are halfway through the first chapter; you will fully understand what I mean. No secrets or surprises, no twisting of plots; just a great little book that was written to help people and also to enable people to help people. I hope you got that.

Secondly, don't look for expert psychological or philosophical advice. Although I have been in the medical field for over 46 years, I am not a doctor, psychiatrist, counselor, or minister. I do however love helping people. I feel in order to be successful in life there are certain precepts that are fundamental and easy to understand. In other words, I don't believe that a "good life" requires weekly counseling sessions. Now don't get me wrong, some situations you encounter may call for just that but most of life can be governed by common sense, conscience, and some of the ingredients that we are going to discuss in this book.

Thirdly, I will not be talking like the head professor in a literature university. I want to reach your heart, mind and soul and believe the simpler we present things, the better we are able to convey the intended meaning. I like plain, simple truths with peanut butter and jelly illustrations.

Lastly, there may be bits of humor laced into the serious content. That does not mean we are taking anything lightly but sometimes a little light heartedness and a laugh is just what the doctor ordered. We will be doing a lot of deep introspection into our lives and at times dealing with failures that produce regret which leads to depression. A bit of fitly placed laughter can break the chain.

As we begin the book you will see a discussion of life's boo boos in Chapter One and what we would just love the ability to do in order to correct them. Towards the end of the chapter we will come across the premise for this book; it's purpose. At this point you may be tempted to put it down and say' "Na, I don't need all this." If you do, please look at the titles of the remaining chapters. I believe your curiosity will drive you to read on. Besides, you already bought the book. You will see many truths that will make you say, "That's right" and "So true." They are not enlightening nuggets that no one is ever thought of before but truths that we do not incorporate into everyday life causing us to make wrong decisions that alter the course of our lives.

The two main purposes for writing and trying to push this book is:

1. I believe without doubt that you will see some truths that can and will change your life.

2. If you are like me, after doing some personal introspection, you will think of others that you can help after putting these things into practice. In a nutshell, I want to be the old man with a laundry list of regrets helping others that are just like me and preventing others (especially younger people) from creating things in their lives that will later lead to regrets.

CHAPTER 1

Reincarnate

HOW MANY TIMES have you said or heard someone else say that they wish they could have one more crack at life? Usually that is implying that if given the opportunity they would live that second attempt differently and have different results. Reincarnation by definition *is "The philosophical or religious belief that the non-physical essence of a living being starts a new life in a different form or body after biological death."* (Wikipedia) In other words after we die, an essence, like our spirit, goes on to inhabit another body or form.

I can remember having very humorous conversations discussing what we would want to be when we came back. One person wanted to be an eagle so they could soar through the skies. Another wanted to be a fish that could swim through the oceans. I remember one wanting to be a squirrel so he could jump up and bite his boss in the nu…. Well, you know.

Then there are those who very seriously believe in reincarnation from a religious viewpoint. Some experience better or worse subsequent lives depending on their actions and lifestyle during the first go round.

1

If I was a terrible human being in my first life, I would start the second life in a much worse condition. (Perhaps a bug destined to rendezvous with a trucker's windshield at 70 miles an hour). On the other hand, if I lived a selfless life and served others the first go round, then I would be rewarded with a much better second life experience.

[PAUSE] Even though we may not accept these beliefs, it may be good to pause here and ask ourselves, "What would my second life be like? Would this life warrant me a better or worse standing in the next one?"

The bulk of us are in a category that is in between these two. Here are our thoughts. "Man, if I could only go back to when I (some event) and do it differently. If I could go back to my twenties, I certainly would have changed a few things. If only I hadn't (had) left, her (him). What was I thinking? Why did I leave (take) that job? Why did I do that?"

We could go on and on. Basically, most of us think of places in our lives where we made wrong choices or decisions. Those that changed the direction our lives took and caused regrets later in life. We end up saying, "If I could only _____". Go back, start over, have another chance at life; you fill in the blank.

In golf we call it a mulligan. You hit a poor shot, say in the woods (lots of personal experience here), so your second shot coming from the woods will be bad. Then because you are trying to catch up, you hit another bad shot and soon you have a terrible hole. You are in the snowman zone (8). So the logical thing to do as you watch that first shot sail into the forest is to say, "Ah, I'll take a mulligan. **Another chance at that first shot** that may produce a drastically different result for that hole. That is really what we would love to have.

If it were reincarnation, then we would have to be specific. "Do you want to come back as a man or animal?

"Well, man".

"Born in this country or somewhere else?"

"Oh, America of course."

"Born to the same or different parents?"

"Well of course, my parents."

So basically, you just really want to come back **as you** and live your whole life over again. Well I have some bad news for you... your makeup and personality will lead you to make the same mistakes and poor decisions as you did the first time.

"Ah, but for the second go round, I want to know then what I know now and be able then to make the right choices and decisions."

3

Oh, I get it, what you really want is a time machine. You want to go back to say July 1986, knowing what you know now, so that you won't make the poor decision to get out of the Air Force with only eight years left for retirement. (Ya, I know, and I have been kicking myself for 34 years now.)

Sometimes it's great to reflect back at the wonderful things that have happened in life. TRUST ME, going down the 'Time Machine' road will only cause regret, despair, and depression. Those thoughts like "If I could only go back and undo what I have done" or "If I could go back and do this or not do that; or say this or not say that; or change decisions on that; or to go here or not go there...."

I have run that road a lot and actually it becomes a bit funny as you start arguing with yourself as to when you actually want to go back. I have gone back as far as 8th grade. The real nonsense part about it is, as we have mentioned, there are no time machines. What we need to do, grab this now, is to stop spending our time and energy musing over the things that we cannot change and invest ourselves in the things that we can. The next paragraph is the one that I told you will actually reveal the truth that this entire book is based on and the one truth that you and I will need to grasp if we want to produce successful lives. It is so simple, and I am certain most of you will say, "well ya, I know that. I don't need to read a book to tell me stuff I already know. I guarantee the rest of the book will cement the truth into your life and you will see the way your life can change.

We cannot go back in time with what we know now and change the decisions and choices that we made in order to erase the regrets we have today. OK. Here it is. We can start living today with a magnified awareness of what caused us to fail in the past showing us how we can succeed in the future.

Let's go back to the golfer (Bob) who uses the mulligan. He hits a poor shot which can really affect the outcome of the hole and even the entire round. He asks his fellow players if he can hit a mulligan. He says to himself, "I know what I did wrong. I took my eye off the ball and raised my head. Great, now he goes back to the tee, keeps his head down and eyes on the ball and hits a great shot. YEAH! Now here is the lesson. We can't go back and do mulligans in life. Life goes on and you have to play your ball from where it is. That is what we can't do. What can we do?

The next weekend rolls around and the golfers hit the course again. As Bob approaches the tee, he NOW has a **conscious awareness** that he is in the same spot he was last weekend. He remembers to keep his head down and his eyes on the ball and he hits a great shot.

A simple way to put it is, he learned from his mistakes. A simple way to say it yes, but not so simple.

How can I prove that statement? How many times do we go through life making the SAME MISTAKES over and over again? That is why it is so critical to develop that awareness and use it all day, every day. In my personal golf game, I would make that same mistake at least ten to fifteen shots a round. I begin thinking about other necessary steps, where I want to land the ball, how hard I want to hit it and yet forget the very fundamental necessity that I was trying to remember.

I was riding with a friend one time. He had earlier told me about having to go to court over a speeding ticket. As we talked, we entered a small town and the speed limit dropped drastically; Bob did not. I kindly told him what the speed limit was and he slowed down. He could have gotten another ticket, making the same mistake again.

As you read over the next few, amazingly simple chapters, you will see how conscious awareness can change your life and help others avoid the road that leads to failure and regret. We will discuss this more in Chapter 2. I want to make this really clear. We only have so many years to live. We cannot regain the years that we feel we have wasted because of past choices and decisions. We can, however, do the next best thing which is to make sure that we profit from the lessons that we have learned and avoid any more regrettable actions.

I cannot list all the specific things that you should do like:

1. Make sure you slow down when the speed limit does or you could get a ticket.

2. If you are walking past an ice cream parlor and you are on a diet, keep walking.

3. Your finances are not so good but you THINK you need a new car. Think again!

But what the rest of this book does is give you ways to create that Conscious Awareness 24-7 so you can make those right decisions. It shows us ways to train our minds to pause, think, and then make a conscious decision instead of just reacting.

CHAPTER 2

Enter Life B (and C)

THE NEXT FEW paragraphs may require a bit more attention than the rest of the book. If you are multi-tasking you may want to hold off for just a few minutes. I have often said that there is nothing sadder than an elderly person looking back on a failed life, full of regrets and remorse. On the other hand, there is nothing more exciting than seeing a young person full of ambition looking ahead to a wonderful life. I would assume that most of us fall somewhere in between. One of the goals of this book is to help people in all stages of their lives become fully energized with a new outlook on creating a much better life in the years ahead, despite regrets over past failures and poor decisions.

The main problem with making poor decisions is that those decisions can actually change the course of our lives. Life is a journey or a direction travelled. Poor decisions and mistakes in life will often change our course and we end up living an entirely different life. If we regret those decisions and actions, it probably means that we feel our original path would have taken us to the best possible life outcome.

Let's label the possibilities, Life A and Life B so we can further illustrate. You are traveling along in Life A with goals, plans, and everything seems pretty optimistic ahead. An event takes place or an opportunity. You make a decision. (You will see, so much of life is decision making. More in another chapter.) It may take hours, days months, or years but in retrospect, you realize it was the wrong decision and you are starting to drift off course. Then it hits you... "this isn't what I wanted. This life is so different from the life I aspired to live. Things started falling apart when I .... Boy I sure wish I could go back and ...." Yes, we know; hit a mulligan.

Now let's look at a couple of truths regarding the new life and the old, desired one.

1. Making a wrong decision or choice doesn't mean all is lost. It doesn't mean that your life is now destined to make a drastic change and you can never live the life you were intended to live.

2. The sooner you realize you made a mistake and make a course correction, the quicker you can get back to the life you want. A lot of times, old man PRIDE steps in and doesn't allow us to make those corrections. "I know what I am doing. I can do what I want to do, it's my life. No one is going to tell me how to live my life." I know that sounds like a teenager talking but you would be surprised

just how far that damaging attitude follows us into adult life.

3. Speaking of pride, in order to make that course correction, you may have to eat a lot of crow, make many apologies and beg for forgiveness. A lot of the mistakes we make are in our dealings with others. Circumstances and the reactions of others often will determine if the correction is possible. Broken or injured relationships can be healed but it takes time to rebuild the trust. Getting back to Life A will require time and patience.

A Couple of Examples:

(Scenario 1): Ted left his wife for another woman and moved out of state. He had his reasons and felt like what he was doing would make him happy. Well, years passed by and that theory was proven wrong. He was miserable; hardly ever got to see his children and one grandchild; and was not happy with his new wife and Life B. His ex-wife remarried and was very happy, the children were all grown and out of the house. Do you think a phone call to the ex with sincere apologies and tearful requests for forgiveness will start a course correction? It may, but I sincerely doubt it. Ted is in Life B and will not be going back to Life A. Some things cannot be corrected or changed. In some cases, Humpty Dumpty cannot be put back together again. So then Ted has to spend the rest of his life miserable and regretting a decision that totally ruined his life. First of all NO, and secondly there is no such thing as a totally ruined life until it is over. (READ ON)

(Scenario 2): Bob and his family are living Life A to the fullest. Bob has a great job and makes good money. They have a nice home, money in the bank and their house is almost paid off. An old friend contacts Bob about a tremendous business opportunity. At first Bob was very skeptical but his friend and others in the business were all wealthy and wined and dined Bob for weeks. He finally gave in, bought into the business with his savings and refinancing his house. His first few checks from business profits were more than he made at his previous job and Bob was sure he made the right decision. Then it happened, allegations of unethical and illegal practices surfaced with ensuing lawsuits. After the smoke cleared, Bob was broke with two mortgages on the house and not a penny of savings in the bank. His wife found childcare for the kids and went to work to help but they were in a financial mess. They were now in Life B because of a poor decision he had made.

Bob also found work but made much less than he did with his original job. He couldn't help but remember how happy they were in Life A. He wanted to go back. Well, there were no time machines so he couldn't go back and undo what he had already done. But Bob was determined. (Remember that word …

DETERMINED). He furthered his education over the next year and a half, overhauled his resume and soon landed the job of his dreams. In a couple years, his wife was able to quit her job and the finances were back in the green. Being back to Life A had never felt so good.

Okay, so now let's look at Life C. It may seem like we are dragging this out a bit but it all comes together in this chapter and then there are a few 'How To' chapters that can and will change your life. To review, Life A is the good life. The life we were destined to live. We followed the right path, made the right decisions, and a basically very happy with life. Now that is not to say that we didn't make some mistakes that could have caused some problems. They didn't however change the course of our lives.

Life B is the life that poor, course altering decisions landed us into. (Scenario 1) It is full of regret and unhappiness, basically a life that is just lived but not enjoyed. There may be some good times and some laughter, but overall it is a disappointment to our life's purpose and desires.

Now Life C. Life C is a purposefully created life, brought into existence by learning from the mistakes in Life A and developing some checkpoints in our lives to stay on course. Life C is for those that cannot make corrections and return to Life A. (Boy I sure hope you are following me.) Determined to live a better life, we cast aside depression and regrets and start to create a whole new life. You can be happy again. You won't ever feel 100% again but boy 95% isn't bad.

Ted in Scenario 1 came to himself, made some decisions and got determined that no matter how rough it had been and no matter how much time had been wasted, what time he had left would be in a life of purpose and happiness. He divorced his 2nd wife (neither were happy so it worked out well) and eventually met and married a wonderful lady. He moved closer to his children and grandchildren so he could see them more often and mended some broken bridges with them. He reincarnated into Life C.

I encourage you to continue on and fully digest the next few chapters. If you are in Life A, they can really provide some preventive measures that will keep you there. If you are in Life B.... good news, you can get out of there and develop a wonderful Life C to enjoy.

We are not only going to discuss life changing items, but things like losing weight, smoking, drinking problems and others. (No don't put the book down. No preaching just some general truths on habit formation). If you love people and want to help the ones that you love, absorb the next few chapters, and share the concepts with them.

CHAPTER 3

Be Constantly Checking Your Autopilot

THESE NEXT FEW chapters will go a lot faster but each has a great truth that can and will help you live a successful life. This one in particular is extremely important and further illustrates an important precept we previously discussed; Conscious Awareness.

Now conscious awareness is not a complicated, psychological term. It simply means being consciously aware at all times of what you are doing, where you are going, and basically all aspects of your life. On the other side of conscious awareness, we have Autopilot. When a pilot puts his plane into Autopilot, the plane just follows a prescribed course and remains at a determined altitude. The pilot then has the plane flying itself.

Life also has an autopilot feature. We call it by other terms such as routines, habits, or patterns. So, there are three statements to start off with examining Autopilot:

1. Things on autopilot can often be good for us.

2. Things on autopilot can sometimes be bad for us.

3. We should CONSTANTLY examine what we have on autopilot.

Regularly brushing your teeth, exercising, reading good books (like this one), and getting a good night's sleep are examples of things we often have on autopilot that are good for us. These are often automatically done without much thought. We get up in the morning and brush our teeth. We eat a meal and brush our teeth. Getting ready for bed, we brush our teeth. It is not something that we normally have to plan or put on our calendar.

It is a very helpful to have as many GOOD things on autopilot as possible. The things that we have to deliberately think about can be forgotten and missed. This is easily seen when we try and start a new good habit. You really need to start exercising so you determine to start walking on Mondays, Wednesdays, and Fridays. Alternatively, you will lift some weights on the other days except Sunday. The first week you do pretty well. However, as Thursday night rolls around and you are getting ready for bed you remember you forgot to lift. It's too late now so you miss it.

You hit the next few days with no problem and then another miss. Until the activities become a habit or routine that is cemented in your subconscious (autopilot), you will have a few misses here and there.

Once it is on autopilot, unless something major comes up, it is usually never missed. Getting as many profitable things on autopilot as possible is a key to a successful life.

Then there is the other side of the coin. Things that get on Autopilot that shouldn't. As someone that battles the weight fight, I can testify as to the harm that simple habits have on trying to lose weight. I don't mind helping clean up after dinner at all but I caught myself, on autopilot now, nibbling the entire time. I tried to balance my portions at meals to keep the calorie count down then while putting the food away I would have a bite here and a bite there and a spoonful here. I never decided as I got up from the table, "OK, I'm going to graze a while as I put the leftovers away." I just did it automatically.....it was on auto pilot.

During the winter months, my other half and I got into another habit. After all the dishes were done, we got things like lunches ready for the next day and then plopped into the recliners and started watching some TV shows we wanted to see. But it didn't end there. Soon we found ourselves just watching whatever was on. Basically, we became evening couch potatoes. As spring and summer rolled around when we used to do things in the evenings, we decided we were too tired from hard days at work so plop, back to the recliners. It wasn't something every night we decided to do. It was just so automatic we did it without thinking. It too was on auto pilot.

Well I finally came to the conclusion that I needed to be consciously aware of what I was doing and decide if I was going to do it. If I was going to change, I had to make some solid decisions and if everything was on autopilot, I did not have control.

My other half is trying to quit smoking. I told her it must be easy because she has done it so many times. Each attempt she claims that the hardest part is getting past the regular times that she would smoke like first thing in the morning, breaks at work, after meals and before she went to bed. Now she smoked more than that but those were her golden smoking times. Not only is she fighting a physical and chemical addiction, but also deeply engrained habits.

She smoked about a pack a day and would stop at a convenience store each evening to get her cigarettes. It was automatic. People who worked there, when they saw her walk in, pulled her brand off the shelf and had the pack waiting for her. Some of you know just what I mean. Now, she is consciously aware that she is trying again to quit smoking and so as she approaches the store, autopilot is off and she consciously decides NOT to stop and buy a pack.

So in wrapping this chapter up, I want you to write down five words to help you with your autopilot;

Conscious Awareness, Decision, Discipline, and Determination. Be Consciously Aware of what you are doing and especially note the things that you have on Autopilot that you are trying to rid yourself of or trying to get on autopilot. Make a conscious Decision to stop the bad or start the good. It takes Discipline to make the change; it won't be easy. And lastly be Determined. Don't let anything stop you from making the change. Determined people get things done.

Look at Olympic athletes. They want that Gold so badly they can taste it. They are Consciously Aware of what it's going to take. They Decide they are going to pay the price. They Discipline themselves. While others are drinking beer and eating cake, they decline because they are in training. When others are relaxing, watching TV and sleeping, they are exercising, working out, running, and practicing their event. They are Determined and nothing is going to come between them and the Gold.

You say, "Well, I'm not an athlete and I'm not going for a Gold medal." Isn't success in your life just as important? I think when it's all over you will agree and be glad you paid the price. It's not easy ..... but it is worth it.

CHAPTER 4

It's All About Decisions

IT IS SO sad and very depressing to regret one's past. What you would give to go back and change various things in your life. "Where would I be now if I had only or if I hadn't....." okay so let's not go there. Remember, NO TIME MACHINES. However, you learned some valuable lessons and they can make you SOOOO successful from here on out. I know in my life and probably yours as well, most of the things we regret boil down to poor decisions or as we will discuss in a minute, no decisions. Now you can't go back and change past decisions, but you can develop a 'Decision Making Process' that will help you make the right decisions in the future.

Let's start by defining a good **Decision-Making Process.** You may be able to add more things yourself but here is the gist.

1. Is this something I actually have to decide on? Sometimes we conjure up scenarios where we feel we have to make a decision and actually none is required. Living by standards and principles helps us avoid many decisions. A man in a junky pickup truck bumped into my car and now there is a big dent. Should I

punch his lights out???? (The most important fact here is "Is he bigger than you?") *Just kidding.* I have principles that I live by and I do not go around and randomly punch someone that has bumped into my car. No decision needed.

2. The **options** in a decision should be clearly defined. Make sure you know EXACTLY what each option is.

3. For each option, you should list **Pros and Cons.** I highly recommend for major decisions to actually write them down so you can see them clearly and not forget something when it's decision-making time.

4. Along with the Pros and Cons, look at the **Short and Long-term** effects of the decision. Instant gratification often clouds judgment and causes poor decision making.

5. You should ask yourself **who** else will the decision affect besides you? Will there be others involved in the result of the decision?

6. Are there people who may be able to help you in making the decision? Perhaps others who have been faced with the same decision and especially others who would be affected by the decision.

7. **When** does the decision have to be made? Sometimes we do have to make snap decisions but most of the time we have some time to run them through this process. Forty some years ago my wife and I were looking at buying our first new couch. It was on sale and we wanted to discuss it since it was a big expense on our tiny budget. I asked the salesman how long the sale was on and he looked at his watch and said "about another hour." He wasn't actually trying to sway my decision but he was trying to pull me away from using the decision-making process.

It is important to realize several things. For example, not all decisions are life-altering decisions. I'm driving down the interstate and see that traffic is slowing down and I see a lot of brake lights. You have been there.... must be an accident. Just ahead on the right, there is an exit. It is backed up and cars are continuing to pile in. Do I get off the exit or stay on the interstate? No time to dial 511 and get more information. Just to be honest, I drive a lot and have faced this scenario many times. Sometimes I stay on, sometimes I get off. Sometimes I chose correctly and other times I did not. The main point here is this is not a life altering decision. You face these situations all the time so we are not going to spend time on these.

Secondly, many of what we call decisions are actually just **reactions.** We don't run it through the decision-making process, we just react. It's an automated response. These can get us into a lot of trouble and may or may not be life altering. Let me stress, **this is very dangerous territory.** Many lives have been ruined and lost due to reacting rather than deciding. Most fights occur due to reactions. People who commit suicide seldom run the idea through a solid decision-making process. Families are broken up, kids get addicted to drugs, people with problems turn to alcohol usually as a result of some type of reaction rather than making decisions.

I don't like to use personal examples but this is a good one. When I was in high school, (several decades ago) I was offered some pot. My friends were all doing it and having fun so I **REACTED** and took a few hits. (Please don't tell.) No harm, no trouble, so no big deal. I joined the USAF and my first assignment was in Spain. Hash was big over there at that time and sure enough I was offered some. Now at an initial briefing, we were told that getting arrested in Spain for drugs could land you in a Spanish prison for 7 years. I **DECIDED** to decline and stay away from those that offered it.

So how do you make sure that you are deciding on important issues? Slow things down and, yes you are correct ...... be **Consciously Aware** of what you are doing. I don't want to ride this pony to death, but I cannot stress how important this chapter is. I don't want you to dwell there but if you look back at the things in your life that are now bringing regret, I feel certain that most of them are due to decisions that you wish you would have made differently.

Please remember the second purpose for this book. I want to help those of us that live with regrets in the past and learn from them to have a successful life from here on out. But also, these truths can help young people avoid the same mistakes that we made. It is just a matter of convincing that child or grandchild that practicing them can save them a world of hurt.

Let me throw one more thing in here for you to think about. Impulse spending is basically a Reaction. I see, I want, I get. What will the purchase(s) do to your finances? Never thought about it. That is what Reaction is. On the other hand, making a budget is a planned way to make decisions on various ways that funds SHOULD be allocated. Can we afford that new truck or that pool? Careful planning and saving and following your budget may make them affordable later.

Let's look at a scenario that unfortunately happens far too often; a real life wrecker. Bob has been married for twelve years and has three children ages ten, seven, and three. He really loves his family but the romance fires have not exactly been blazing in the last couple years. He had to go out of town to a seminar. (if you are thinking ahead, you are right) As he was eating supper at a little bar, he notices a very professionally dressed, slightly younger woman glancing at him.

A stirring starts within Bob and it worsens as she approaches his table.

"You here for the leadership seminar?" she asked

"Yes I am."

As she sits down, she continues, "Me too. I really thought that main speaker last night was great. Brought out a lot of good points."

You guessed it. The conversation continues over a few more drinks and then she invites him to her room for a nightcap. Bob's head is reeling. It won't hurt anyone if they don't find out. We are miles from home, so it is safe. This will kind of fill in the gap for the lack of sex I am getting at home. Basically, Bob is in reaction mode and trying to justify his actions.

He returns home and it was a bit awkward when he first sees his wife and kids, but he got over it. He did feel a bit of guilt, but it dissipated pretty quickly once they settled into their routines.

Then it happened; an email; from the mystery woman; then another, then they started coming daily and more than once a day. Fast forward a couple weeks and Bob is in the position where he has to tell his wife. You have heard the expression, "going to hell in a hand basket." That pretty much described Bob's life over the ensuing months. The woman he loved was hurt beyond words and cried for weeks becoming so depressed. The family life was destroyed and the kids that could understand what was going on were devastated.

The end result was shame and dishonor in the community and a bitter divorce with ensuing serious financial problems. Bob was so sorry, mostly over the hurt that he caused for his wife and children. He is older now, lives in another state, hardly ever hears from his kids and grandkids, and is alone having been through a few failed relationships.

The one thing Bob does do is wish every day that he could go back and reverse that terrible decision to hook up with that other woman. But we know it was not a decision, it was a reaction.

Let's rewind a bit. As she sat at his table flirting with him, he starts the Decision-Making Process. Pros, Cons, short-term, long-term, who will it affect? Basically, he would have come up with this DECISION, "One night with this woman is not worth even a chance that I could lose my family and wreck my home."

Slowing things down eliminates rash decisions or reactions and a solid decision-making process can and will save you trouble and later on down the road.... regret. REMEMBER: There are no time machines.

CHAPTER 5

Checkout Time

WHAT ON EARTH do I mean by 'Checkout Time?' The checkout counter is where you pay for the items that you want to take with you. Everything we have talked about so far is extremely valuable in living a reincarnated life, a better life. It is basically based on **past** life experiences that have given us the foresight on how to live the **present** so that we can enjoy the **future**. But like everything that is valuable, it comes with a price. Now I guarantee it is worth it; but it does cost you. The concepts are very easy to understand, but not so easy to put into practice.

If you are a young person reading this, you may find it a bit easier to employ the things we have talked about. For example, you may not have as many bad habits on auto pilot that have been there for many years. It is easier to remove something that you have been doing for a year and as half than it is something that you have been doing for 30 years. Ask any long-time smoker that has attempted to quit.

Our brain develops pathways when we do things. The more often and longer we do something the deeper and more defined the path becomes. A family moves into a new house and the family dog loves running around the inside perimeter of the fence. The first few times he does this, you can hardly see the track he was running on. After a month or so, there will be a well-defined path. A similar process occurs in the brain as the same activity is repeated over and over again.

Here is Jane. She is 47 years old and is significantly overweight. She is not in very good physical condition, tires easily, and has very little energy especially later in the day. Her evening routine for years has been to finish cleaning up after supper, heading for her recliner and watching TV the rest of the evening. One day, Jane picked up and reads this wonderful book entitled "Reincarnate Now," (just had to get a plug in there) and decides to make some changes. She thinks to herself "Instead of plopping into the recliner after supper every evening, I am going to go for a nice long walk." She even purchased a treadmill to walk on when the weather was bad.

She was excited and had a pleasant walk the first evening and the second. She was tired when she returned home and a bit sore the next day, but she felt good. She went again the next few evenings but somewhere around a week later she found it was a bit more difficult to go. That recliner and remote looked inviting and the initial excitement had worn off.

Then the voice in her mind began talking. I'm sure you have heard the same voices. "It won't hurt just to take one night off. It looks like rain and that treadmill is so boring. I'm not sure it's doing any good anyhow." **NOTE:** This is the point where you will determine how successful your *reincarnated life* will be. This is where you pay the price. The place where you do what you don't really want to do but know you need to do or vice versa. Don't do what you really want to do because you know it isn't right. KEEP on walking! DON'T PICK UP that cigarette! READ that good book. LEAVE those potato chips alone. I think you get the idea.

Now this is a key point in determining the success you will have during the rest of your life.

1. You are going to look at changes that you need to make in your life so that you can enjoy the Plan B life we discussed.

2. You will be excited about those changes and excitement will carry you through the first week or so.

3. After that initial period, the excitement will begin to fade, and you will find it harder to stay on course.

4. ***** NOTE***** (This is probably one of the most important truths in this book) At this point you have to trade the faded excitement for DEDICATION and DETERMINATION. You are no longer doing or not doing it because you are excited or its fun or you like it but

because you NEED to in order to make that change.

Can you see the 3 distinct phases? EXCITEMENT... DEDICATION ... AUTO PILOT. The second phase is so important and varies in duration. Some things take a shorter period of time and some things take years or even a lifetime. I know people that stopped smoking years ago that claim they would still love to have one. I can't stress enough how huge this transition is. Think about it. How many dieters keep the weight off? How many people quit smoking over and over again? How many Gym memberships are created in January (New Year's resolutions) and are abandoned in the next couple months? How many treadmills are now just places to hang shirts? What happened? The excitement wore off, it was not replaced with dedication and determination, and so .... End of story. That's all she wrote!

One more thought along this line. Do you think champion athletes like eating properly while friends pig out at the buffet? How about getting up at 5 a.m. to work out or run while friends sleep? Do you think they enjoy hours and hours of practice doing the same thing over and over again? I think the answer would be a resounding NO. But they do it. WHY? Because they traded their initial excitement for dedication and determination, and they are champions; **and you can be a champion too!**

I hope I didn't insult your intelligence when I was talking about decision making. You have to admit that most of our regrets do come from improper decisions made in the past. We have to pay the price here as well many times. We have to trade "I want" for "What is best?" I want that new truck, but what will that huge payment and increased gas money do to my budget? I would love that new job but what will it do to my family if we move to that location? I hope if anything that a caution light comes on in your brain when you are about to do something without really employing a solid decision-making process. Just really think it through and please remember this very proven truth; **Accepting short term gratification WITHOUT considering long term effects often result in disaster and eventually regrets.**

I have heard accounts of athletes who were on their way to the major leagues, expecting a very promising career. Unfortunately, they were sidelined due to a blown knee or a severe shoulder injury. They now have to resort to Plan B. Now they may feel bad about that over the course of their lives, having missed that great opportunity. However there are no associated regrets because what happened was most likely not in their control. But you can control what you do and the decisions you make. Take the time and effort to choose wisely and you will continue following the course of your successful life.

CHAPTER 6

Reincarnate NOW!

OH MY. I shudder as I begin this chapter. This is probably the hardest chapter to emphasize enough and to put to practice. I would not have written this book if I did not think it could help both young and old make some significant changes in their lives that will produce happiness. Just writing these precepts down has been a tremendous asset to my life and has helped me talk more effectively to my grown children about their lives. Nothing in this book or any book will do anyone any good unless at one point in time they START. No one has ever won a race without starting.

Here we are at the Olympic one-mile run. The starter raises his gun and BOOM, they are off. One runner says, "No need to rush things. Think I'll go in a little bit." How often have we decided on things that we need to start doing or stop doing and really get firm about doing it but then put it off. Tomorrow, next week, at the beginning of the month, January 1st. Soon days become weeks, then years and we look back and regret not starting "NOW!" That runner will not win, and neither will you or I, if we don't stop procrastinating.

Just an example, I saved this topic for this chapter since it is so time sensitive. It is so important to start investing money early. I have spoken to so many people that want to retire but can't afford to. They are not financially able because they failed to start saving at an early age. Like so many things, procrastination causes regret. "Why didn't I start saving sooner?"

Since time is the key element in investing, let me share an illustration. Assuming 8% interest, someone at 25 years old, investing $200 a month would have accumulated almost $703,000 by time they are 65. Wait one year and it drops to $677,000 losing $56K for waiting one year. Wait five years, and it drops to $462K. As amazing as it may seem, starting at 35 instead of 25 (waiting ten years) will cost you $402,000 in interest.

We have discussed getting rid of bad habits…. start now. My other half always has a reason to delay her efforts to stop smoking. I have been with her for 16 years and she was trying to quit when we met. That is 16 more years of tar and nicotine in her lungs. She has now been smoking for 32 years. I dread the thought but someday she could be regretfully wishing she had stopped many years ago.

Don't wait to stop smoking. Don't wait to start dieting. Don't wait to start exercising. If you decide college is the best course for your life, start now. Decide you need to apply for a different job, do it now. Need to tell that special person how you feel about them, do not put it off. There are three little words that will help procrastination produce regrets in your life.... "as soon as." I will stop smoking as soon as I finish this project at work or get a new job. I will start dieting as soon as the holidays are over. I will start investing as soon as I get these bills paid off. I will start college as soon as I get some money saved up. I will start exercising as soon as the weather gets better.

Procrastination puts a carrot in front of you that you will never catch. Let's use that last line as an illustration. It's early spring and the scales are revealing that winter has not been kind to you. You decide to start a walking routine as soon as the weather gets nice. The weather gets nice and the walks begin. Summer comes and now it's very hot, so procrastination changes the carrot. I'll start back again when it cools off a bit. Fall arrives and it cools off and the walks resume. You guessed it. Winter comes and it starts all over again.

What is the alternative???? When the weather is not nice, use that treadmill that is just being used to hang clothes on or go to the mall and walk around briskly for a while. Here is a funny story. I was at my son's house a while back and we were discussing why he wasn't going to the gym anymore. He stated that he just didn't feel like driving into town to work out. I noticed a pizza box on the counter. I asked if the pizza place delivered way out there and he admitted to driving in to get it. You see, you will make the drive if you really want it.

I cannot stress this point enough, but I don't think I really have to. You know how quickly time goes by and how short life really is. If you are still young, it may not seem like it now but trust me it does. Someday, if you don't believe me now, you will wish you would have. Why do you think so many of us that are up in years would pay anything for a real time machine; one reason would be to get back some of the time we lost.

I have one last personal illustration on the subject of procrastination. I got into a tremendous business opportunity over 20 years ago. Over the course of my life, I started and quit five times. I kept coming back to it because I really believe in what we do. In this business, we need to get prospects, make appointments, etc. I have a tracker that starts on one week and goes out several months to track each week's activity (contacts, appointments, etc.). I can not tell you how many times I have put new dates into that chart as I would "start again."

Meanwhile, I constantly read about those in the company that have reached financial independence. Many of them started on day one and worked hard for seven to ten years and have reached their goals. They have all of the money and residual income they want and need so they are done. I look at myself and wonder where I would be with my goals if I had not procrastinated for so many years. Yes, I am starting again TODAY!

Many car accidents occur because of drivers improperly negotiating turns. People traveling too fast or waiting too long to make their turns often find themselves totally off the road or worse. Huge ships take almost three miles to completely turn around. If they are heading for troubled waters, they must start their turn very early to make the turn. Life is a huge ship. Don't wait too long to start turning.

CHAPTER 7

The END.........or The Beginning? Your Call!

WE HAVE REACHED the final chapter. Believe me when I tell you this, I am not so nearly concerned with how well you liked the book but rather what you can do now to improve your life. Seriously, I would rather be contacted by a few folks who would tell me that somehow, this book benefitted them than 1,000 people telling me how great a book it was. Its purpose was not to propel a writer to the Best Seller list but one human being that has been through it trying to help other human beings that are going through it.

I am convinced that understanding the concepts and putting to practice the things we have discussed will indeed help you successfully manage your life. If you are living in regret over past mistakes, put a smile on your face and begin the reincarnation process, take one step at a time. Don't expect overnight wonders to occur. It is a process and takes time. I assure you that it will not be easy. I wrote these things and believe me; I have to fight every day to stick to my guns. It is not easy, but I guarantee it will be worth it.

There are so many people living what I call 'wrecked lives'. Lives that could have been better had things occurred differently. Some of those things were not controllable. Disease, accidents, fires, hurricanes, and car accidents do come our way and can make devastating changes to our lives. It is amazing though how resilient the human spirit is though as we seem to be able to recover from these uncontrollable events. An inner strength comes to us and we rally to overcome them.

The most crushing event that I ever encountered happened back in 1999 when my oldest son (21 at the time) died suddenly from no apparent cause. I went to work on Christmas Eve at 5 A.M. At 8:30 a.m., I got a call that he was unresponsive and not breathing. By the time I got home, I could tell he was gone. The pathologist that did the autopsy told me that in 1% of the deaths they encounter, they can never determine the cause. I was devastated and could never imagine recovering. It still hurts to this day, but life went on. The strength came and enabled us to keep on living. Many of us faced terrible events in our lives that we had no control over. I hurt over my son's death but there are no associated regrets because it was not under my control.

On the other hand, there are several things I did in my life that I do regret. Mistakes and poor decisions that I made that caused my life to make turns in the wrong direction. Many, if not all of you, have done the same and it is for all of us that this book was written. How do we rebound? How do we overcome? How can we live a happy life with all the regrets we carry?

STEP 1: Dump the load that is weighing you down. As you attempt to create and live this new, reincarnated life, there are things that will help your journey and things that can stop you dead in your tracks. Imagine preparing for a long hike up a beautiful mountain to get a splendid view from the top. You start at the bottom and fill your backpack with very heavy rocks. Although you can barely lift it, you manage to slip it on your back and start your journey. Obviously, you just made the journey a very difficult endeavor and you most likely will not make it. Depression, guilt, regret, and despair are all those rocks and they will keep you from reaching your destination. You will start, tire, and eventually quit. Stuck right where you are, in a life where you are not happy. On this particular journey, you will need every bit of energy you can muster. Those rocks will zap away the energy you need to reach your destination.

STEP 2: Take the things with you that will be beneficial. Instead of rocks, you carefully chose the items that you carry in your backpack. You put a flashlight in, and some water, energy bars, some rope, and a flare. You also take a compass and some maps of the area. These things will all be beneficial to you on your journey. Checking to see what you have on autopilot, a solid decision making process, and a clear cut path that has taken others to the top are all things you need to get you to the life that you desire to live.

STEP 3: Most of all be determined. Don't let anything stop you. It will be a fight, but you can do it. As we mentioned before, changing your life isn't easy but it is worth it. Whatever you need to change in your life, it will be a fight; don't tire and never quit. My dad took me fishing one day when I was pretty young. I hooked a pretty big fish. I started to crank that thing in as hard as I could. My dad told me to just let it swim around for a while. Sure enough, it swam up and down the river a bit. Soon, there was little resistance on the end of the line. It was hooked, it fought, tired, and eventually quit; I then easily reeled it in. Reading good books, listening to good tapes, developing, and keeping a positive mental attitude will give you all the strength you will need to succeed. And remember Step 1, don't let past mistakes and regrets hook you.

CONCLUSION

I KNOW WHAT living with regrets can do to you. I know what living a life that you feel you were not meant to live is like. I have felt the pain of depression and despair. I have had long periods of time where my life was full of "If I only hadn't...." or "If I only had...." and particularly "If I could only go back to ......" I realized however that none of those thoughts were good for me and got me absolutely nowhere. I needed a new life, one that I could live after learning many lessons in the past. I hope these lessons will help you as well. Live that reincarnated life. Life is short my friend, don't waste another day. You CAN DO it!

ABOUT THE AUTHOR

ALLEN DAUGHERTY SERVED in the USAF for 12 years and has been in the medical field for 46 years. He has also been very involved in counselling youth and adults. Working with a large financial services company, he educates the public in financial responsibility and retirement planning. His theme: He loves helping people.

Printed in the United States
By Bookmasters